You Can Be Debt Free

How to Get Out of Debt and Stay There

Dr. Gary Webb

PublishingPoints
Author Services

Dalton, Georgia

You Can Be Debt Free

ISBN-13: 978-1522954057

ISBN-10: 1522954058

Disclaimer

This book is designed to provide only general information on debt reduction. This information is provided and sold with the knowledge that the publisher and author do not offer any accounting, legal or other professional advice.

In case you need for any such expertise, consult with the appropriate professional. This book does not contain all the information available on the subject. This book has not been created to be specific to any individual or organizations' situation or needs. Therefore the content is necessarily general.

Every effort has been made to make this book as accurate as possible. However, there may be typographical and or content errors. Therefore, this book should serve only as a general guide and not as the ultimate source of subject information. This book contains information that might be dated and is intended only to educate and encourage you to live a more fulfilling life.

The author and publisher shall have no liability or responsibility to any person or entity regarding any loss or damage incurred, or alleged to have incurred, directly or indirectly, by the information

Table of Contents

You Can Be Debt Free

Dr. Gary Webb

Dr. Gary Webb

Introduction
Debt and Excess Weight?

I recently lost over 50 pounds using an approach that I believe will help me keep that weight off permanently. Why? Because I've changed many habits that had caused me to become over about 60 pounds overweight. In fact, I'm still using those principles and habits and expect to do so for the rest of my life. I still hear donuts calling my name when I go near a bakery, but that's okay. We're not friends anymore. I may eat one or two through the year, but it's not that likely. I can't afford it. I can't afford to make stupid choices about my weight. Can you?

I mention this because I see a great similarity between weight and debt. It has been quiet a while since I was overwhelmed with debt. It wasn't a happy time. My wife Jane and I had a hard time digging our way out of that hole.

Today, I realize that my weight gain and my debt problem both came from my carelessness. I was careless with my health, and I was careless with my finances. I ate just because I felt an urge, not because it was within my nutritional needs. I spent money because I had a craving to get something, not because it was within my income limits.

The comparison is obvious. When we eat more calories than we burn, we will gain weight. When we spend more money than we earn, we will gain debt.

So, I believe some of the same principles that helped me lose weight can help you to get out of debt and stay there. They are exactly what I did years ago when my wife and I had accumulated a substantial debt while I was in the Navy. The comparison with being overweight just makes it clearer.

Why Do People Make Stupid Decisions about Money?

Look around your community. Have you seen those signs for payday loan companies? These are the worst of today's loan sharks. They sell themselves as being concerned about your lack of money, but if that were the case, they could simply pay your bills for you. Instead, they set up contracts to insure that you are paying them. The racket is, they have to pay back right away after payday or else pay a huge interest rate that will rob them for months to come. Can you say, "Road to poverty?"

Why do normally smart people make dumb choices about debt? Part of the problem is that people try to get the most pleasure as quickly as possible. It's a short-term mindset. That wouldn't be so stupid if you knew you were only going to live till the money and credit ran out. However, those who enjoy living beyond their means may not live very well when those means fail. In other words, if I spend tomorrow's income today, I may have nothing to spend tomorrow. Individuals, families, and even nations make the same mistake.

That same short term thinking causes many debt crises. For example, they fail to do minor repairs to their homes and cars, resulting in major expenses that could have been avoided entirely. They go into debt, sending a child to a major university rather than insisting that they attend a local community college that offers similar programs for a fraction of the cost. Rather than packing a nourishing lunch to take to work, they buy junk food at the over-priced convenience store or fast food restaurant (both of whom accept credit cards).

They destroy their health trying to save money, even though health care will cost them more later and may deprive them of the ability to make a living. Many who have tight budgets will neglect preventive medical care like dental checkups, vaccinations, physicals, etc. As a result, their medical problems are more frequent and often more expensive. Since these were "unpredictable" expenses, they feel justified in putting that medical bill on their credit card or allowing the hospital to set up a payment plan.

Some of the same people say they cannot afford to join a fitness club. Then, they spend twice that amount on cigarettes. Which decision is most likely to be moving them deeper into debt?

Sometimes, we make decisions today because we have false as-sumptions about our future. Perhaps we believe we are going to inherit a large sum in a few years. That can cause us to avoid saving for retirement, college expenses for the kids, or to buy a car. That false belief seems to justify our decisions, at least until it doesn't come true.

Many people assume that they will be making more income in the future than they do today. That's a fairly common and reasonable belief, but not always true. It could be that our health declines so that we cannot do the same kinds of work. Our company may go out of business so that we lose a position that would be hard to replace.

We could enter into a recession where jobs are lost and incomes actually decline.

Financial wisdom is a rare thing. People often make bad decisions when they are under financial pressure. It's amazing to me that those who waste the most money on lottery tickets are those who are barely making ends meet financially. They may fall behind on their monthly bills because all the money was spent on these tickets immediately after payday. Financial expert Dave Ramsey calls state lotteries the "stupid tax." I agree.

Some people even make decisions under the influence of alcohol or drugs. Perhaps others do it due to peer pressure that they didn't have the courage to resist. Their friends won't help pay the debt, but they may be the cause of it.

Don't be stupid about your money. There must be a better way to spend your money than paying interest to someone who is already rich. Some of the rich people get there by collecting interest from people who are too stupid to ever be out of debt. Don't let that be you!

In Over Your Head? Stop Digging!

Do you really want to get out of debt? We've discussed how you got there. We all did it the same way. We spent money faster than we made it. If you are ever going to get out of debt, that habit needs to change immediately. You must determine to start living within your means. In fact, if you are going to get out of debt, you will need to live on less than what you are making. You will need to spend less right now so you can pay off what you spent in the past. Make sense? I hope so. If it doesn't, you can stop reading right now because you have just decided to stay in debt.

Debt problems are simple. The problem has two parts: income and spending. To get out of debt, at least one of them must change. Usually both must change to some degree. Either income must increase, or spending must decrease. Or both.

When you have a rising debt, it's time to quickly understand what's happening. Which is easier for you, increasing your income or cutting back on your spending?

The Need for More Income

If you only have enough to buy enough food to survive, then it's obvious. You would need more income! So let's assume you are on the verge of starvation and work from there. We're assuming none of your spending could be reduced. If so, you can't get out of debt without making a larger income. That's what I call a no-brainer!

So, how do you solve that problem? I don't have all your answers, but let's take a few moments to look at some of the basic alternatives.

You could ask for a raise. If you are making your boss a lot of money by your good work, but getting paid very little, this might work. If you are doing such a good job that you would be hard to replace, he might be afraid to lose you to one of his competitors. In some cases, he might even be afraid that you would go out and become one of his greatest competitor. If an employer is able to pay you what you know you are worth, then you might need to start searching for a better employer. I'll need to save that for another book!

If your employer is not able to pay you more, it is possible that you are not producing enough for his profits to increase. That may not be his fault or yours. It could just be a bad economy or perhaps the field is over-crowded for your area. If that is the case, you may need to **consider a change of occupation.** It might even require getting more education or training in order to do a different kind of work. Your state employment office may have counselors available to help you make that type of decision. Otherwise, a community college may have counselors who can advise and/or test you to find out your aptitude for a particular field.

Another way to increase income is with **a second (or even third) job**. We are now in an economy filled with part-time jobs. Some don't pay very well, like fast food restaurants. Others pay much better than you might expect. Several people I have known were making over $1500 per month, working part-time, delivering pizzas. Bizarre! I guess some folks think they have money to blow. While they are spending themselves deeper in debt because they didn't think ahead to get the pizza, you can make money to get out of debt. Some guys **begin a side business**, like lawn care. It doesn't cost all that much if you already have a good riding mower. It actually pays pretty good if you don't try to undercut the price everyone else is charging. Some people make pretty good cleaning houses, or even better by cleaning businesses at night. Another friend did pretty well by detailing cars, right at people's homes. The interesting thing there is that he was using the client's water to wash the car and electricity to run a vacuum and buffer. All he had was a truck with cleaning supplies and equipment. While there, he would offer to make their foggy headlights clear. Rather than use expensive supplies for that, he used off-brand toothpaste and finished it with a silicone polish.

You can be innovative and start your own business. Some people find that they make more in their part-time personal business than they do while working for someone else.

If you work a commission job, you might find some ways to **make more sales** - which would probably mean working longer hours. If you are hourly, it is still possible with some employers (such as construction) to **work overtime**.

Another way to increase income, at least for one month, is to **have a garage sale** or to list some larger items for sale in the paper. My wife and I had a garage sale every week for several months while I was in school in Missouri. I'm still a little ashamed to admit that we picked up old furniture along the road, fixed it up and sold it. One garage sale netted us $1200, our highest ever.

Ten Benefits of Living Debt Free

These are not the only benefits you'll have once your debt is gone. You might even be able to add to the list right away. What are your dreams that can only be fulfilled after your debt is gone?

1. Great flexibility in spending and saving.
2 Ability to save for a good retirement.
3. Gives a peace of mind for considering wise investments.
4. The ability to take more vacations and spend more time with family.
5. Money that is earned is managed more tightly than money that is borrowed.

6. Being debt free allows you to bargain for better deals by offering cash.

7. Being debt free means you get to buy or save with money that was wasted on interest.

8. It means you can afford to take action immediately when a bargain or a great investment comes your way.

9. Debt free living produces less stress. Stress is a leading cause of health problems including high blood pressure, diabetes, and cardiovascular problems.

10. You can afford to be generous in meeting the needs of others.

Chapter One
How Much Do You Need?

Life does not consist in the abundance of things that you possess? Do you believe that? Jesus said it, so I certainly hope you trust Him with something this important.

How much stuff do you need? Think this question through because it is important when we consider the issue of debt. If you have an exaggerated sense of need, you'll spend all of your earnings quickly and without much thought. That is the road to poverty. Believe me, poverty is when your most essential needs are in danger of not being met. You may be unsure of whether or not you'll have enough to buy groceries, to pay rent, or keep the lights on.

According to the CNNMoney American Dream poll,[1] a quarter of Americans believe it would take between $50,000 and $74,999 to live a happy life. Almost as many, 23%, said that it would cost them between $100,000 and $199,999 per year to live that good life. American author, Henry David Thoreau said it well, "That man is richest whose pleasures are the cheapest."

Having more money doesn't produce happiness. Having more of what money can buy won't satisfy either. What is no one would love you unless you paid them to do it? Would that kind of love make you happy? But what if you believed it could? You'd spend all you have trying to buy something that money can't buy. Money can buy sex, but not love. Money can buy companionship, but not love.

Most people are spending more than they have to buy things they cannot afford to please people who cannot be pleased. Don't be one of them.

Take a moment to do a simple exercise. Get two pieces of paper. Make a quick list of the ten things you can least do without. In other words, the ten most important necessities for your survival.

Got it yet?

Okay. Now take that list and put the items in order. You can work it from either direction. When you look at the list, you might immediately see one that you could easily do without. Or from the other direction, you might see one that is the very last thing you would want to try to live without.

Now, think a moment about how you are spending your income. Your income represents your time, the little pieces of your life that you are either investing or wasting each day. Does your spending line up with what you have written on the second piece of paper? Are you neglecting something very important because you've already spent your money on something else?

Managing money is about priorities. Take a look at Appendix One. It would be good for you to work through that process even before you begin to examine your monthly budget. Could you do that?

Why Get a Mortgage?

It should be obvious that I want people out of debt. That doesn't mean that I'm hostile toward ever borrowing. Borrowing has some dangers, but it does also have some potential advantages - at least in some situations.

Most people are older before they learn to manage money well. As a result, their best way to ever own a home is to get a mortgage. A mortgage is often a very good financial proposition. It often works out cheaper than paying rent, at least after the first few years, and at the end of the time you own the house. It's almost a no brainer, if you have the salary to afford it.

The problem is that most of us do not understand the difference between taking out a loan to buy an asset that will increase in value, like a house or perhaps a business, and getting credit for things that will never again be worth what we paid for them. That includes cars, furniture and all the little things that we put on our credit cards.

Remember though - every debt, even a mortgage can go wrong. It carries a risk just like credit card debt. Thousands of people lost their homes and all the money they had invested during the recent recession. When their income fell apart, most didn't even have an emergency fund to help them through a few months of hard times. They could only accept the inevitable foreclosure.

Three Approaches to Paying Off a Debt
The Worst Way Out of Debt

I would like to say any way out of debt is a good way, but that's not true. Many people try a way that often leaves them deeper in debt instead of getting them free. What is that dangerous path to being debt free? Debt Consolidation Loans!

Take a moment to think about that term: Debt Consolidation Loan. The goal of Debt Consolidation Loans is not to get out of debt quickly. Why? The longer you are in debt the more interest you'll be paying to the company that gave you the loan. What they offer is lower monthly payments - not quick debt reduction. The fastest way out of debt is never by making lower monthly payments. Ever!

Some Debt Consolidation Loans are extreme rip-offs. They can be worse than a bad pawn shop. I've seen people go into one of these loans where they pay a higher rate of interest than what they had on any of their previous debts. If you were to calculate when that loan would be paid off, it could be as much as 20 years later. Seriously? Is that what you want?

What do I think of this strategy? Let me be clear. Warning! Danger! Stop! Dangerous Curves! Hazardous Materials! Is that clear enough? I've never seen a good situation for a debt consolidation.

One of the problems of Debt Consolidation is that it sounds so good to the desperate. It sounds like a way to make life easier, but it is deceptive. Debt Consolidation allows you to keep your debt, if you like it. It also allows you to pay smaller payments each month without dealing with your real problem: overspending. Debt Consolidation can allow you to go even deeper into debt because you have lower monthly payments right now. A few months down the road, you will have added more debt to what you had and the payments will be out of sight again.

The Ladder Method

This approach to getting out of debt is rarely the quickest, but it is sometimes the cheapest. I've never used it because it would always have taken me too long. The goal of the Ladder Method of debt reduction is to pay the lowest amount of interest - not to reduce monthly payments or get out of debt quickly. Now just think for a moment. Often, the difference between interest rates isn't that huge anyway. If you can get out of debt quicker, you might actually save more interest money as a result.

Here's how the Ladder Method works, if that's what you decide to do. First, you look at your credit cards or other debt statements to determine the interest rates being paid. Then, make a list of your debts with the highest interest debts on top. Now, start paying off your debts, paying as much as you can, on the biggest debt first. When it is paid, put as much as possible into paying off the second largest debt, and so on, till you've paid them all.

The Snowball or Pyramid Method

I started off calling this method the pyramid method. Dave Ramsey calls it the Debt Snowball. I'll confess, I like his name for it better because it's so easy to see how a snowball grows as it rolls downhill. The goal of the debt snowball approach is to get out of debt fast. The primary thing isn't having lower monthly payments or avoiding the most interest - just getting out of debt completely and quickly.

In this book, we are going to use the Debt Snowball approach. Why? We are not looking for an easy way out of debt. We are looking for a way to live completely free of debt, beginning as soon as possible.

Chapter Two
Five Steps to Get Out of Debt Fast

Many people want to get out of debt. Most want to do it the easy way; so ten years from now, they will still be in debt. Some want to get out of debt by inheriting a fortune or winning the lottery. Sorry, but the chances are greater for them to be swallowed up by a hole opening up in their parking lot.

Most people who are in debt today will die that way. I'm not being a pessimist. It's just reality. And I don't want that for you. You and your family deserve better. If you are a Christian, I can say that the Lord wants better for you. But it will require a wisdom that most people just can't seem to grasp.

Living in debt is the result of poor financial habits that are seldom broken. Until it is far too late, borrowing seems easier than planning ahead and making wise choices. It definitely seems easier than having to wait to satisfy those impulses to have more and to have it now!

If you want to get out of debt, I recommend that you do it as quickly as possible. Don't sacrifice your health or the health of your family, but get out of debt quickly. Make it a priority so that you can live in a freedom and joy that others cannot imagine. Do it so that you can give generously -- not just have good intentions. Do it as quickly as possible so that you can avoid wasting years living in financial bondage.

Let's Begin That Journey with Five Simple Steps

I certainly do not mean that they are simple to do. That's a lie. If you are accustomed to digging yourself deeper into debt, it will seem hard to start filling that hole. It will violate all those deep emotional habits that have perpetuated your behavior. **Let's get started!**

#1 Stop borrowing money

If you want to get out of debt fast, you have to stop using debt to fund a lifestyle that is above your means. This says, no more financing furniture, no more signing up for credit cards, no more test driving brand new cars that you can't buy with cash. We will focus solely on the debt that you currently have so that you can develop a game plan to pay it off quickly.

If you have any credit cards that are maxed out, cut them up. At this point, you can't use them anyway. As you begin to dig your way out of this mess, however, every card you've paid down will become a temptation. From your past history, you don't handle that kind of temptation very well. Am I right? Go ahead. Admit it.

You cannot decrease your debt while also increasing your borrowing. **Stop borrowing. As soon as you finish the next step, cut up all of your remaining credit cards.**

Just in case I didn't make myself clear: Stop Borrowing Money.   Don't use your credit cards ever again!   Don't spend as much as you make!   Quit digging the hole deeper!

#2 Start a basic Emergency Fund of at least $1000

How does a person who is in debt pay for an emergency? You know the answer, don't you? They go deeper into debt, usually with a credit card. If you really want to get out of debt, you will need a reserve fund that takes the place of that credit card. That will keep you from making dumb choices under pressure. Put a buffer between you and debt; that is exactly what an emergency fund does.

What is an emergency fund for? For emergencies only! It isn't a savings fund for something that was predictable, like your car needing new tires. You knew those tires would need to be replaced. If you look at them, you can even make a wild guess about when you'll need to go shopping for new ones. However, you might not be able to predict that the transmission on your seven-year-old car would fail this week. That becomes an emergency that will probably knock out the full emergency fund in one blow!

Let me just warn you. If you have a substantial debt, and you decide to work your way out of it, you will have at least one emergency sometime during that period. Without an emergency fund, your whole debt reduction plan could be hijacked. You could then become discouraged and give up. Don't go there!

To begin with, a $1000 emergency fund will cover most of the common emergencies people have. It could include the deductible on an auto accident or replacement of a water heater that goes bad. These are completely unpredictable expenses that you cannot usually pay from your monthly budget.

Later, when all your revolving credit is paid off, you should consider a major emergency fund that would equal three to six months of your income. That amount could require a lengthy period to save, but it would be your protection during times of sickness or unemployment. Workman's Compensation seldom pays enough for people to meet normal expenses. As another possibility, you could have several $1000 emergencies, one after the other. The major emergency fund would protect you from going into debt under those circumstances.

Action Step for the Emergency Fund

As soon as you have the basic emergency fund complete, take a step of faith and courage. Cut up all the credit cards. Don't apply for new ones.

#3 Set Up a Sensible Budget and Stick To It

A budget is a plan, written down in advance, of how you are going to allocate your next month's income. That definition has four parts.

First, it is a plan. For some people, a budget is a record of how you spent your money. That's not a plan at all. Some people have considered their checkbook or their bank statement as their budget. That information is valuable to help you plan a budget, but it isn't a budget at all.

Second, a budget is written down in advance. Before the first income for the coming month is in your hands, you need to write out a plan for how it is to be used. A budget should outline exactly where every penny is going to go. You may need to adjust it if you miscalculated, but you shouldn't deliberately have any large "miscellaneous" category where you have no idea about how it will be used.

Thirdly, a budget should show how your income will be allocated. Allocated isn't a common word any more. Its definition is easy to remember because the word "located" is in it. Your budget should tell you where every penny will go. Where will it be located after it leaves you? Will it pay the power bill or buy groceries?

Fourthly, a budget is for the coming month. Weekly budgeting is almost impossible because most bills are monthly. Some are actually quarterly, semi-annual, or annual. If you have some of those longer-term items, it is good to set aside some money each month toward paying those expenses when they come due. That way, you don't have an "emergency" of stupidity. You saw it coming like a train coming down the track. But you didn't do anything about it - like getting off the track before you become hamburger. No emergency is foreseeable.

It Starts with Income

A sensible budget begins with your income. It is a plan for how you are going to use every penny even before you get it. That income is the limit for your spending. Your task is to decide what portion of that income will go for your basic living expenses, how much to get out of debt, and how much for saving.

Those decisions are primarily a matter of setting priorities. What is most important to you?

Having a budget to track your income and expenses is crucial to getting out of debt fast. It will help you spot funds that can be diverted from careless use into paying down your debt. Needless to say, if you are in debt, you can't afford to be careless with how you use your money.

Your budget will reveal whether you have a surplus or a deficit. If your regular bills and living expenses are less than your income, that's a surplus. If they are more than your income, it's a deficit. Your goal is to increase your surplus by increasing income and/or decreasing expenses. That surplus is not "extra money". It is your tool for getting out of debt.

Set Your Priorities

Your budget is not my budget. It is your plan to fulfill your purposes.

As we have been discussing, getting out of debt is a fantastic plan.

Record Your Plan

You may want to keep your budget in a spiral notebook or three-ring binder. For the tech savvy, you might want to build it with an Excel spreadsheet. Or maybe you'd like to try out a simple tool that is on-line. It is found at www.mint.com. This website has just what you need to track your budget. It also can be set up to import your bank account and credit card information.

Next, go over each item in your budget and ask yourself, "How can I make this amount smaller?" One way is to cancel services that you rarely use or could do without such as Netflix or magazine subscriptions. It could be money being spent for a higher cost plan at the gym. It could mean cutting back on eating out in restaurants. The more committed you are to getting out of debt quickly, the more you will be willing to give up some of the luxuries in life. Sometimes, it may mean getting the same or similar goods and service from another source. You may cancel an expensive fitness club member-ship and join the low cost one down the street. Look on the Internet for some bargains, introductory plans, or coupons to help reduce these costs. If necessary, completely eliminate the most costly, but least useful items.

#4 List All of Your Debts - Smallest to Largest

At this point, you need to take a look at how you have been spending your money. That's not your budget, it's just history. However, knowing your history should help you plan for your future. Look over your checkbook, bank account statements, credit card statements and the like. Start looking for places you could have done better - expenses you could cut out. You might decide that you could brew a pretty decent cup of coffee at the house rather than stopping off at Starbucks on the way to work. It could be a habit change. You could start taking a small cooler to work filled with cans of Coke instead of buying five a day from the vending machine. It is likely that you'll find some waste in your history. But your history doesn't need to become your future.

As you review, look for items that might need to increase. Let's face it, your budget should help you build a better life. It shouldn't make you miserable. Let me go back to what I've learned while dieting. If I make my diet too tough, too limiting, I will begin to resent it. I'll hate the diet so much that I can't resist that King-Sized Snickers waiting for me at the grocery checkout registers. We can actually make our budgets so tough that we are stirring up a sense of frustration and a feeling of "doing without." When that happens, we are likely to see something we really, really want. It could even be a budget busting credit purchase that makes our goal even harder to reach.

#5 Put as Much as Possible into Your Smallest Debt

Got that? You've listed all your debts from the smallest to the largest for a reason. You are going to target one debt for extra

attention (and extra money) until it is paid off completely.

There is no such thing as "extra money." All money has a purpose, even if you don't know what it is. I believe God has a plan for our finances - if only we learn to cooperate. It can be part of our relationship with Him.

The unexpected money that occasionally comes into our lives could be for a future need. If you don't have your basic emergency fund complete, then apply that money toward it.

Your budget should include using non-essential, or unbudgeted money toward getting out of debt FAST. If that is your goal, then do it with all your heart and mind.

If you can find some place to trim your budget this month, don't act like it's "extra money." **If you can save money on your clothing budget, spend it on getting out of debt.** If you can stop eating out so much (not essential), then put those dollars into paying down your debt as soon as possible.

When the smallest debt is paid, you can add that monthly amount to minimum payment of the second smallest debt. Did you get that? That second smallest debt is now the target of all your efforts. If your income tax refund check comes, it should go on paying down that debt! It isn't "extra money." It is part of your plan to get free from debt ASAP. If grandma sends you an unexpected birthday gift, you know where that goes, don't you? On the targeted debt!

If you have the opportunity to make some additional money during this period, do it, but don't waste it. Put it into the war on debt. Pay as much as possible off the smallest debt every single month. Get aggressive with destroying that debt, and you'll discover tremendous freedom. Along with a well-managed budget, you have the freedom to do things you could only imagine right now. You'll be able to get better deals on things by bargaining for cash. You'll be able to travel, to get more generous with giving, and be more confident about your future.

You'll Probably Blow It Some

I'm not sure what to say here. I don't want to say, "Oh, that's okay. We're only human." **I don't want to make your mistakes seem unimportant.** It could be the beginning of a really stupid habit. But it probably isn't.

You will make mistakes. Fact. Then what? As soon as you know that you have spent too much or done something else that hinders getting out of debt, just stop digging that hole. Don't beat yourself up. You've been making some good progress. One mistake will slow down your goal, but it isn't going to stop you. Somebody else, maybe. But not you! You know what you want, and you know how to get there. So get up and get started again.

Think about the mistake only to plan how to avoid it in the future. It is history. **History is only useful to plan the future.**

John was recently divorced. She got custody of the kids, and custody of a big chunk of his income. He kept custody of the health insurance payment for the kids, the payments on both cars (including the one she continued driving), and custody of over $40,000 in credit card debts. When we first met, it was because he had changed jobs to make more money. The new job required lots of travel, so he traded his car for a newer one that could get better mileage. Doesn't sound too bad, does it? Not until you realize that he was upside down on the old car. That is, he owed more on it than he could get in trade. He felt like the car dealership was doing him a favor by adding that difference to his new car loan. When he also saw the increased premium for his insurance and found out that the MPH was not as good as the sticker said, he panicked. He came to me for help. He had blown it. It was a serious mistake, but not fatal. It just meant he had to set up a tighter budget and pay less toward his debt snowball. It was going to take him ten years to break dig his way out. Unless, he could increase his income.

Yes, you will probably blow it. Probably not as badly as John did, but you too will find a way out. **Don't allow yourself to accept financial slavery!**

Chapter Three
Other Ways to Eliminate
Debt Quickly

I've said that getting out of debt and living debt free isn't easy. Some of the tips to follow may look like they are easy until you try to implement them. They are ways to reduce debt without all of it coming from your paycheck.

None are automatic, but in some situations, they become essential. We won't be able to go into any of them in depth, but I'll try to give you some direction to find out more. In fact, I may take up some of them in another book. Let's get started.

Consolidation Loans

As stated previously, I strongly oppose debt consolidation loans. I do so for several reasons.

The first is almost too basic to mention. **You will never get out of debt by going into debt. A debt consolidation loan is just that - a loan.** It adds extra interest to your existing debts. Usually, it makes it appear like a bargain. What they do is to give you a smaller interest rate, one that is at least smaller than the highest rate you are now paying. After all, they are getting a new customer. You will be paying interest to them instead of someone else. They will offer you lower payments. You know what I think about that. If you've forgotten, look back at Chapter One when I discuss the three approaches to paying off a debt. Read about the worst approach.

Companies often attempt to get you to **consolidate unsecured credit card debts by establishing a second mortgage or refinancing your house through them**. Man, that's a great deal, isn't it? It's great for the loan company because they are unlikely to lose! You, on the other hand, could lose your house because you've been stupid with credit cards. **Don't, please don't do this!** Sometimes, they will try to get you to consolidate your credit card debt by taking out a loan using your car as collateral. Again, they win, but you could lose big. Others will have you borrow against your whole life insurance cash value or against your 401K. Warning! These could be hazardous to your financial health!

Another disadvantage of having a secured loan debt consolidation is that you will often extend the amount of time you'll be making payments. In other words, **you are setting up a plan to stay in debt longer. That could mean that you end up paying more interest than you would have on those high interest credit cards.**

A few companies still offer unsecured debt consolidation loans. Very few. These loans at least have the advantage of not risking your property or other assets. It is usually offered at a lower interest rate than the credit cards, because they don't allow you to keep adding more to the loan every month. This is still bad medicine for your debt sickness. It will reduce your monthly payments (not your total debt). By doing that, it will cause you to suddenly start receiving special credit card offers in the mail. They can give you the impression that you can afford to go buy something on the card. **Remember, that**

old credit card debt didn't go away. It's just hiding inside your new debt consolidation loan.

Consolidating your debts into a single loan with one lower monthly payments may give you emotional and financial relief. However, it may also let you feel prematurely confident about your financial situation. That could become your downfall. It could cause you to qualify to go even deeper into debt that you were when you felt you couldn't afford to pay your power bill. Over the long term, you will then pay a greater portion of your income as interest to those strangers in suits who don't care if your kids have enough to eat.

Negotiating and Settling with Creditors

When you have been overwhelmed by debt for a long time and have gotten behind on your payments, this could be a part of your way out of debt. Since you have a history of not paying and are now living on a budget, it won't be hard to convince your creditor that you are unable to make the full payments on the debt.

It may be that they have some alternatives that will help. It could be that they offer to reduce the interest (or even eliminate it) if you will resume payments at a reduced rate.

If you fail to make payments, sooner or later, you will receive a letter. So, it is often better for you to contact them before that letter comes. By doing this, it will reassure them that you aren't trying to skip out on the debt.

Before making contact with your creditor, make a list of all your

debts (you should already have that if you have been working through the previous chapter. Look over the list to see which you can pay regularly and which you can't. You probably will find that some aren't a problem, but others are beyond your reach.

It may be that **some will be able to reduce your interest if they learn how bad your situation is.** They may allow you to **take a break for three months**. This can be good if you are having a temporary problem such as recovering from a period of unemployment.

When you call them, it is important for you to **make sure that you are talking with someone who has authority to approve changes to your debt payments.** Explain to the first person who is on the phone that you need to speak with someone who can approve a reduction of payments or approve a lower interest rate. Explain what you would like to request, but don't get tied down with someone who can approve your request. That's just a waste of time since you'll need to go into detail with some in authority.

You are not the first to request a favorable change in your debt payments. They will be more comfortable that you are. They will just be glad that you aren't trying to dump them or file bankruptcy. They will be happy to work with you to find the best way to eliminate the debt. It may be that they would be willing to reduce the debt by as much as one half if you will send a substantial part of it immediately. If you can afford that, do it.

They do have the power to take you to court or to hire debt collectors who will sue you. However, that is a last resort for them. They don't want to risk losing it all by having you file bankruptcy. Then, the entire debt could be discharged by a judge.

Whatever is agreed to on the phone, ask them to send you a written copy either in a fax or email attachment. Get that written agreement before you send any money.

If they have agreed to a payment adjustment, you can be sure that they will be watching your account even more closely. **If necessary, you can contact a local branch of Consumer Credit Counseling Services to ask them to negotiate for you.** You can contact their international offices at (866) 531-3433 or their website. They may be able to negotiate a discounted credit card settlement for you.

Refinance Mortgage for Lower Rate

Advantages

A refinanced loan may have a cheaper interest rate. That has been especially true in recent years since the beginning of the 2008 recession. Right now, someone who borrows $100,000 could save themselves as much as $100,000 in interest over the life of a 30-year mortgage. Generally, it is thought that you should refinance if you can lower your interest rate by more than 1%. That isn't absolute, however, because of other factors. For example, how long are you planning to stay in the home? Are you converting from a fixed rate to an adjustable rate? By the way, it is good to go from variable to fixed, but not the other way around!

It may have an improved loan period. By "improved", I don't mean longer. That would just keep you making payments longer and in debt longer. What I mean is shorter and at a better rate. Often the interest rate on short-term loans is better. You could save thousands in interest payments by doing a 15 year refinance instead of a 20 or 30 year one.

Negotiating a refinance loan is going to be easier than your first mortgage. Why? You have more leverage. You have no time pressure. You can walk away from any deal. They know that, so they work hard to get your business.

Many people need to refinance now to escape a variable rate mortgage. Since the rates are now low, do this as soon as possible. Rates are unlikely to stay this low. Even if you need to raise your payment just a little, at least it will be fixed from now on. You won't have to worry about how the variable rate payments will skyrocket when the economy changes.

Consolidate your first and second mortgages into a single mortgage. You know how I feel about debt consolidation. However, this is one situation where it might work. Your property is already the collateral for both these loans. Your interest rates for one or both may be higher than the current available rates. You can arrange to have the loan period be no longer than the shorter of the two mort-gages. If all those are the case, you should definitely consider it. Before acting, you might contact the Consumer Credit Counseling Service that I mentioned in the previous section. They would be able to run the numbers for you. Then, you'll know how to negotiate with the lenders.

Downsides

There are some potential downsides to this approach.

The lender may want to add some "garbage" fees. You would expect some reasonable fees to reprocess and approve the loan, but some lenders want to add others at the last minute. Be sure that you have a good faith disclosure of all the costs of the loan before you make your decision about which lender to use.

It could change your mortgage to a "recourse loan." In some states, your initial mortgage is considered the absolute full collateral for the loan. If you default, the mortgage company can foreclose and seize your home. But they cannot come after you for additional money if they can't get the full loan value out of selling your house. By shifting over to a refinanced mortgage, that may change this status. Then, after a foreclosure and sale of the home, if it doesn't pay off the old mortgage balance, they can seize other assets to make up the difference. Ask the Consumer Credit Counseling Service or your state housing finance agency about the status of your state laws on this issue.

Your original loan may have prepayment penalties attached to it. You should check the Truth in Lending statement to see if this applies to your original loan. There is a way around this in many cases. If you are refinancing through the original lender, they may waive this penalty in order to keep your business.

You may become less flexible in your location. Why? Well, since there are refinance charges and fees, it will usually take about three years for you to break even on the cost of the new mortgage. That means you should not refinance if you expect to be moving within the next three years.

It only helps those with significantly higher interest rates. Many people who have bought homes within the past few years were able to get really low interest rates on those loans. To refinance now, wouldn't save much on the monthly payment, but it still would have the extra fees added into the principal of the loan.

Refinancing your mortgage could be a good choice to shorten the time you will be in debt and to make paying off other debt more affordable. It is at least worthy of some thought.

Negotiate Lower Rates on Home Equity Lines of Credit

If you already have a home equity line of credit, then you may want to contact the lender to see if you can renegotiate the loan. Let them know that you could do it through other lenders, but that you have been happy with their service so far. Then see what kind of an interest reduction they can offer.

Do not use your line of credit to do anything other than what is needed to preserve the value and livability of your home. In that case, the interest from this loan will be a tax deduction from your federal income taxes just like the mortgage interest.

Get Lower Interest Credit Cards

I'm not in favor of credit cards. They are a temptation too strong for me when I'm under pressure. Since I still don't have a large cash reserve, I could turn to a credit card for "help in time of need." In other words, I would get a long term, and expensive solution to a short term problem.

However, I believe I'm writing to people who already have those cards in their wallets. Since the interest rates on existing cards has risen so much in recent years, getting a lower rate can save a lot on interest payments. If you have a good credit rating, you can get a lower rate card. In addition, you may qualify for a zero percent balance transfer. This could allow you to go for a year without interest on that balance. When doing a balance transfer, be careful about transfer fees that charge a percentage of the total balance to make the transfer.

If the transfer fee is small and the rate after one year is lower than what you paid for your old card, you've made a good decision.

Here are some suggestions. Call the toll-free number on the back of each of your credit cards. Ask for customer service. Ask if there is anything you could do to lower your current rate. Most of the time, unless you already have bad credit, they will be more than glad to help you.

If you are carrying high balances on your other cards, and have already paid off the smaller ones, It could work for you to transfer the balances from all the cards onto the lower interest one. Add up all your payments to these cards for the past month. Do not reduce the amount you are paying on each card. Instead, keep paying the full amount that you paid last month for the various cards into this single card. Since less of it will be going for interest, you'll get out of debt quicker. By continuing to pay the full amount, you will also not develop the bad habit of paying as little as possible each month.

Government Assistance

Somebody may be telling you that the government has a program to help you pay off your credit cards. Don't fall for it. There are no such programs or grants available for individuals. The government only uses your tax dollars to help the big banks who lend you money. Does that sound sarcastic? Well, you are very perceptive!

Grants

The government won't help you because you are in debt, but they might have another reason to help. You might qualify for a grant for another purpose that who also benefit you financially. For example, they offer grants for education (which could help you qualify for a better paying job).

The government may have grants for developing your small business, if you have one. Find out more at www.grants.gov. They have them for disaster relief through FEMA. That could make a world of difference if you've lived through a tornado, flood, forest fire or hurricane. Overall, more than 26 government agencies offer grants of some kind that are available to individuals - but not for the purpose of getting you out of debt.

Loans

The government does have loans for individuals, if you qualify. You could get a loan at a much better rate of interest than you would pay with most credit cards or commercial loan companies. These are not for debt relief, instead they are usually for specific purposes such as business, housing and education (student loans). Many of these loans are not directly from the government. Instead, they are administered through local banks. You can find more information about these loans at www.govloans.gov.

Some advertisements on the web or on TV make it appear that a particular debt relief organization is connected to the federal government. Usually, these are just crooks who are trying to bait you into their schemes. They know how to generate a false confidence in order to get their hands on your assets. They get richer. You get poorer.

HARP
Before moving on, I do want to mention one government program that may be able to help you keep your home if you are in financial trouble. The Home Affordable Refinance Program (or HARP) was established after the last recession to provide assistance to homeowners in danger of losing their homes. This is a very useful program, even though they don't give you a penny. You can find out more by calling (888) 995-HOPE) or at their website MakingHomeAffordable.gov. There's a wealth of information there.

Bankruptcy

When it comes to debt, the court of last resort is bankruptcy. Here, a court declares that you cannot afford to pay your debts and that you will not be able to do so in the foreseeable future. It is a severe process where you agree to give up everything that you own in exchange for being released from all your debts. The court will decide what each of the creditors will be paid from what is paid from the liquidation of your assets. The federal government as well as all of the states and U.S. territories have bankruptcy laws.

In most states, a bankruptcy court will allow the debtor to keep some assets. They are considered to be exempt from seizure by bankruptcy. It is beyond the scope of this book to discuss all the various state laws.

A few states even allow the bankrupt debtor to use the federal bankruptcy exemptions. These include specific amounts, such as the following:

- $22,975 of equity in your home (not rental or investment property)
- $3,675 for your motor vehicle
- $1,550 for jewelry
- $12,250 aggregate value ($575 per individual item) on household goods, furnishings and appliances, clothes, books, animals, crops, or musical instruments
- $2,300 for tools of trade, including implements and books
- Health aids, such as wheelchairs or oxygen concentrators.
- Life insurance policies that have not matured except credit life insurance, and $12,250 in loan value of life insurance policy.
- Retirement accounts that are exempt from taxation, which usually include most genuine non-fraudulent retirement accounts, are fully exempt. However, there is a cap of $1,245,475 on IRAs and Roth IRAs.

There are other exemptions under federal law. For more information about Federal Bankruptcy law see the full tex^{2}t of 11 U.S. Code § 522.

Two Types of Bankruptcy under Federal Law

Chapter 7

Chapter 7 bankruptcy is often called *straight bankruptcy*. It is available to both individuals and businesses. When the assets have been liquidated and creditors have been paid, the remaining debts are cancelled.

Some financial obligations are not removed (or discharged) under chapter 7. These include:
- Alimony and child support
- Drunk driving judgments and criminal fines or restitution
- Debts incurred by fraud or intentional wrongdoing
- Back taxes under 3 years old
- Student loans
- Recent purchases involving substantial amounts
- Properly executed contracts involving titles or liens such as land or automobiles.

There are several reasons of situations when you might choose to file a Chapter 7 bankruptcy:

- If you have no hope of repaying any debts
- If you have debts with no co-signers
- If you are being sued by creditors
- If you need to protect your exempt property and income sources

- If you don't qualify for Chapter 13 bankruptcy.

Chapter 13

Chapter 13 is often called *reorganization*. It reorganizes debt to be settled over a three to five year period. In Chapter 13, the debtor reaffirms some of the debt -- from 10-100%. The percentage will depend on income, nature of debts owed, and the amount owed. Some debts cannot be completed removed or discharged. These include:

- Alimony and child support
- Drunk driving judgments and criminal fines
- Student loans

That is one reason why student debt is such a serious issue today. Young people who are graduating college are often unable to find a good-paying job. But the student loan payments must still be paid! They may lose a house, fall behind on other payments, but not Sallie Mae! Some have said that nothing is certain but death and taxes. Notice that under Chapter 13, back taxes can be discharged, but not student loans! For those who take out a loan for school, maybe nothing is certain but death and student loan payments!

Bankruptcy doesn't carry much of a stigma today because so many have been forced into it in the past few years as they have lost jobs and homes. It is a last resort because it will damage your credit for years. But let's face it, if you are going to live debt free, you might not care much about your FICO score!

Your greatest protection against bankruptcy is a strong Emergency Fund. If you had three to six months of your income tucked aside for an emergency, it might prevent many of the risky situations of life. I know one may who spent six years building up his fund. What happened? The recession. He lost his job. Unlike many, he took a lower paying job almost immediately, The emergency fund help that transition. Today, he makes more on this new job than he did previously on the old one. His Emergency Fund is back up to a six month level again. I wish I heard more stories like that. Don't you?

Chapter Four
Avoiding Debt for College

I'm going to finish this book with a look to the better future that you and your children will have. It is so important that you invest in yourself and in the next generation. College or technical training is one of the best investments you can make. But many people also have found paying for this training very difficult.

Some people have come to believe that debt for college is inevitable. Nothing could be further from the truth. In fact, the more our government encourages students to borrow for college, the more rapidly colleges raise tuition and other expenses. That's my opinion, but it is also supported by the dramatic rise in tuition following changes in federal student loan provisions in 2009.

As noted in the previous chapter, student loans are not discharged by bankruptcy. Under current rules, monthly payments are capped at 10 percent of a borrower's disposable income and forgives the balance after 20 years of payments. If the student debtor does not pay for 270 days (nine months), the loan will be in default. That's frightening because the penalties can include garnishment of paychecks and tax refunds or even Social Security payments. You don't want to go there!

The best time to deal with student loan debt is before it happens. Here are some suggestions to help you get your education without also getting deep into debt.

What's Your Degree Worth Compared to Its Cost?

Consider education an investment. The key question for an investor is: "What is the ROI?" ROI means "return on investment." Regarding education that translates into another question, "How much will my income increase because of spending money on this degree program?" Let's face it. If you get a degree in advanced basket weaving, you shouldn't pay more than a few bucks for the diploma. It is almost worthless. However, many technical and engineering degrees or medical degrees will definitely drive your income higher. Some degree programs won't do much to increase your income, but the degree won't cost you much. Or, you might want to use the degree in a way that reduces the debt, such as teachers who get a loan forgiveness of $17,500 if they teach in certain low income schools.

Choose an Affordable College

If your field of study is available through a public college or university, that will probably be the cheapest route to a degree. Some fields such as ministry, chiropractic medicine, or homeopathy are not going to be available through public schools. However, some of those programs still require the same general education courses that are offered through your local community college. Some fields often require or favor a graduate degree. Those seeking to go into a profession, for example, will often need to get a bachelor's degree as a prerequisite to entering a good graduate program. A lot of money could be saved by taking this path: 1) community college, 2) instate university, and 3) graduate school.

For public education, a great deal can be saved by choosing to attend an instate public university instead of either an in-state private university or an out-of-state university. Out-of-state tuition can add thousands of dollars to the cost, plus travel expenses will increase as well.

Be sure to compare schools on a fair basis. If expensive college is offering a high level academic scholarship and/or grants, it might cost less than a school with lower tuition. Also consider the total cost of housing, fees, meals, or miscellaneous items when comparing schools.

Look into College Scholarships

Scholarships can help you stay out of debt because they don't have to be repaid. There are at least five different kinds of scholarships that may be available: academic, athletics, character, minority scholarships, and for field of study. You might also investigate to see if your employer, church, or community organizations offer scholarships for which you might qualify.

Look into Various Grant Programs

Like scholarships, grants do not have to be repaid. Most grants, especially for undergraduate work, are based on the financial need of the student. The federal government offers Pell Grants, Federal Supplemental Education Opportunity Grants (FSEOG) and the Teacher Education and Assistance for College and Higher Education grants (TEACH) To find out more about these programs, contact your school's Financial Aid Office or through the Department of Education website.

Investigate Work Study Opportunities

Back when I was in school, the work-study programs were mainly working in the university cafeteria for minimum wage. Things have changed. Today, the schools often have connections with corporations or other businesses so that a student can work part-time in the field of their major. This gives better pay and also gives experience that will look good on a resume later.

In addition, upper-level students often have the opportunity to pursue summer internships with companies that pay very well. These companies give internships with hopes of keeping the best and brightest students after graduation.

Can't Find a Job - Create Your Own

If you can't find a well-paying job that fits in with your schedule, you might need to create your own business. Depending on your abilities and resources, you might begin a landscape business, a freelance graphics business, a proofreading business, or tutoring local students in elementary or middle school. You should expect to make well above minimum wage with any of these.

If you pay for college before you get there or as you go, that's great. Any amount that you don't have to borrow is a great advantage for after graduation. Here's another point. I've seen college graduates who were offered a great opportunity with their dream job, but they couldn't afford to take it because of the debt payments they needed to make. If you have little or no debt after graduation, you will not

52

have such a limit. Many of the best entry level jobs don't pay much because they don't have to. They are such a great chance to grow and learn that they have hundreds of applicants for that job. Those who are in debt will just have to pass on that wonderful first step to success.

Appendix A
Setting Your Priorities

This worksheet can help you think through your material priorities. It can be especially useful for couples who need to identify why they struggle with one another to establish a budge.

Rank by Priority (1 to 14)

_____ Food

_____ Housing

_____ Clothing

_____ Medical & Dental Expenses

_____ Transportation & Maintenance

_____ Entertainment

_____ Education Expenses

_____ Savings

_____ Insurance

_____ Charitable Giving

_____ Grooming/Beauty Care

_____ Gifts for friends & family

_____ Retirement/Long Term investment

_____ Furnishings

What are some items that are "budget busters" (items that are under-funded or completely neglected until they are an emergency)?

Appendix B
Your Budget Worksheet

Since it would be difficult to see this worksheet in an eBook, I am going to provide you with a link to it from my website. Just go to http://bit.ly/1NF0h41 and download the file. It is in pdf format so that you can use it on the widest range of devices.

You can also get access to more books and resources for financial growth by subscribing to my newsletter at http://publishingpts.net. It will be especially valuable to those who work at home or are authors.

If you have specific questions related to getting out of debt, you may wish to contact me directly through my email address: gary@mgwebb.net.

Appendix C
Ways to Balance Your Budget

1.   Shop for cheaper insurance. Consolidate auto, home, and life to get a better deal.

2.   Shop for cheaper cable/satellite TV. Don't do a long contract. Re- negotiate at end of each contract period.

3.   Use your cell phone, but get rid of the land lines.

4.   Go through all the items you aren't using. Do a garage sale to trim back. You'll have more room, plus have money to go into the emergency fund or to pay off debt more quickly.

5.   Buy store brands at grocery store. Use coupons for brand name items.

6.   Get haircuts at a cheaper place.

7.   Go to matinee movies instead of regular price. If you are a senior adult, get that discount. Do not buy concession items.

8.   Get books from the library instead of buying from a store.

9.   Join Costco or Sams to get bulk food items. Get a used freezer to store more food.

10. Avoid eating out. It's bad for your waistline. If you must do it, don't order beverages. Just get water.

11. When you do eat out, skip the soft drinks and sweet tea. Stick

with water. It will save you money and also save your health.

12. When eating out, split an entree with someone else. Another thought: just order an appetizer. They are often large enough to be filling.

13. Shift to healthier breakfast foods. Go for oatmeal, eggs or fruit instead of boxed cereals.

14. Go on a budget plan with your power company. Having the same monthly bills will help you balance your budget easier.

15. Christmas is coming. Set a limit in your budget for how much to spend for each person. Set the amount before you choose the gift.

16. I get my haircuts at the local beauty college. Since I bought their annual discount card, the cuts are just $2. That let's me also be generous in tipping.

17. Instead of paying someone to do things like babysitting, handyman tasks, house cleaning, or lawn work, find friends who would be willing to trade one task for another.

18. Learn to make gifts at home. It could be baked goods, craft items, sewing goods, etc.

19. Consolidate your errands to conserve gas.

20. Try having family get-togethers at meal times. It can seem like eating out, but it also allows for either a potluck sharing of favorite foods, and time to enjoy being together.

21. Instead of a gym membership, you can often borrow exercise videos from the library. Go on eBay to get some bargains on simple resistance bands.

22. Make your own coffee at home in the mornings instead of buying

Starbucks on the way to work.

23. Pack your lunch for work. You can even use leftovers at times. Pack some fruit to make it healthier. Maybe include some inexpnsive snack items to tide you over during the day. That's cheaper than the vending machine.

24. Install a programmable thermostat and use it to save money on electricity bills.

25. Stay out of malls unless you are there to buy something on sale. Don't look around, just buy the bargain and leave. Mall rent is very high. Merchants add that to the regular price of most items.

Another bonus idea: Give generously. You cannot out-give God!

Notes

_____

[1] CNN/.ORC Poll money.cnn.com/2014/story-supplement/cnn-orc-poll.pdf. Accessed November 18, 2014
[2] www.law.cornell.edu/uscode/text/11/522. Accessed November 18, 2014.

www.ingramcontent.com/pod-product-compliance
Lightning Source LLC
Chambersburg PA
CBHW061447180526
45170CB00004B/1603